# The Map to
# Clear Messages

*Conversations with a Wizard and a Warrior*

## Nadine Udall Fischer
## &
## Brian Baldinger

with

Deb Stec        Joy VanSkiver

Noble House
Baltimore, Maryland

# The Map to Clear Messages

Library of Congress
Cataloging-in-Publication Data
ISBN 1-56167-839-2

Library of Congress Card Catalog Number:
2003097961

Second Printing

Published by

8019 Belair Road, Suite 10
Baltimore, Maryland 21236

Manufactured in the United States of America

# Dedication

*To Mia Joy, P.J. and Lonne.*
*You are the light of my life. In being given the*
*gift of raising you, I have loved and learned*
*more than I ever dreamed possible.*
*You were not born of my genes and blood but of*
*my soul, heart, and spirit.*
*I will always love you unconditionally.*
*Motherhood is what I have most treasured.*

*Nadine Udall Fischer*


In Memoriam
To Tom Landry,
one of the ultimate influences and
mentors in my life.
He lived his life with three priorities: God,
family, and football. Tom Landry lived his
beliefs and left us that legacy.

Brian Baldinger

# Contents

# Acknowledgements

*I have had the privilege to work with
extraordinary leaders. Your integrity inspires
me. You have challenged me to become
more than I ever imagined.
This book belongs to all of you.*

*Deb Stec for her support in bringing
this project to completion.*

*Joy VanSkiver for her patience and ground
work on this project.*

*My parents...the greatest gift you gave me was
the faith and belief that lives inside.
It has sustained me always.*

*St. Mary Medical Center and its entire staff.
Most especially Dr. Robert Buckman, Director
of Trauma and Dr. John Newsom, VP Medical
Affairs. You saved my son's life.
I will be forever grateful.
Nadine Udall Fischer*

To everyone who has helped me during my
transition from professional football
player to professional broadcaster —
this book is for you.
Brian Baldinger

# Introduction

Nadine Udall Fischer is a corporate communications expert who has worked with thousands of executives since she founded NADIA Communications, LLC in 1988.

Brian Baldinger is a network television broadcaster for Fox. He was an offensive lineman with the Dallas Cowboys from 1982 to 1987, the Indianapolis Colts from 1988 to 1991, and then the Philadelphia Eagles from 1992 to 1994.

Nadine and Brian met when he sought out her coaching to become less of an in-your-face offensive lineman and more of a camera-ready, professional broadcaster. They have worked together for almost eight years.

In this book, you will "hear" from Nadine in a script typeface. (*Nadine is speaking.*) Brian's part of the dialogue is in a standard typeface. (Brian is speaking.)

# Preface

Welcome to our conversations!

We invite you to imagine sitting with us in a comfortable room just chatting about easy ways to communicate effectively with others and with ourselves.

Experiences in the business and sports worlds form the basis for this user's manual to your internal, truly personal computer. Just as everyone takes time to learn how to operate hardware and software, we need to learn how to operate our language and ourselves. We *do* have the power to realize our communication potential.

Making the complex simple, not the simple complex, is our philosophy. You may be surprised, in fact, that the prescriptions we offer are so basic and so simple. We know they work because we've seen the evidence, not just in our own lives but in the lives of the people we coach.

While we put this book together, the two of us learned from our own dialogue. Although we have worked with one another for almost eight years, we found new territories that we had never thoroughly explored. Creating *The Map to Clear Messages* has resulted in our personal resolutions to change, to improve, to enhance the way we communicate every day.

We hope our simple suggestions do the same for you.

*Nadine Udall Fischer*          Brian Baldinger

# What Language Do You Think In?

With persistent work and effort, hard won knowledge may be acquired and then shaped into creative and useful ideas. Often when presented to others, there is a lack of interest with little favorable response. The message given may be of significant value, but failed to be fully understood, nor light the flame of enthusiasm. The message was there, but the messenger failed to deliver it.

Effective, motivational explanations of ideas and concepts, especially complicated ones, are formidable challenges in any sphere of life. When it fails in the business enterprise, as it so often does, the toll it takes is enormous. The success or failure of many people, programs, or even companies, hangs by the thin thread of clear and cogent communication.

Nadine Fischer's new book ought to be read by business leaders everywhere, and by all others who want to feel the magic of being able to touch others' hearts and minds. Nadine is a master. I'm glad to have learned from her. So will you.

Curt Clawson
CEO
Hayes Lemmerz

1

*Everyone has internal dialogue. That little voice that silently speaks to us. This becomes the language that we think in...and that language creates meaning for ourselves, our lives, and for others.*

*Have you listened to yourself lately? Did you like what you heard?*

*Nadine Udall Fischer*

# What Language Do You Think In?

When I interviewed Tmanga Biakabutuku from the Carolina Panthers a few years ago, he explained to me that his native language is French, but he also speaks English and two African dialects. It impressed me that he had four different languages he routinely conversed in.

When I asked him, "What language do you think in?" he said he thinks in French. So, when he's playing football with teammates who only speak English, he's thinking in French. They don't know he's thinking in French because he communicates to them in English!

*"What language do you think in?" was an interesting question you posed. We are totally unaware of what someone else is thinking, and yet all of us have an internal dialogue going on all the time.*

*The language we think in creates meaning for ourselves and our lives. It's not just what we think in order to speak, it's what we think when we send messages to ourselves. For example, when something negative happens, what is our internal dialogue? What are we saying to ourselves? I heard this phrase going through my*

*mind recently: "You're just a joke." Years ago, that would have made me feel a little down, but this time I stopped and said, "Where did that message come from? Where did I ever hear that message that it would automatically pop up like something pops up on a computer screen?"*

*I was able to recall why I heard that and decided I didn't like having that phrase come up automatically. I've learned to become more aware of what I'm saying to myself.*

*Human beings in general have a lot of messages that run through their minds. It's our own <u>intrapersonal</u> language; it's not inter — between two people — it's intra, what we're feeding to ourselves.*

How does that language get there?

*Think about how you learn a foreign language. What's the best way to do that?*

I don't think any of the methods they teach you in school really teach you how to speak the language. They teach you to conjugate verbs and learn vocabulary, but you never really learn until you go to the country, until you're forced to speak it. Learning a new language is more than speaking it, it's thinking it, it's feeling it, it's listening to it. There has to be total absorption. You become immersed in the culture and you hear it over and over again.

*I agree with you. I've taken Spanish, and I've taken a little French, but there's nothing like being immersed in the culture. Let's say we're in Spain for three weeks and there are certain phrases that are repeated over and over again. Those are the phrases that are top-of-mind. Those are the phrases we learn.*

*That sometimes happens with negative phrases, too. If someone says something negative to you over and over again, those messages can become top-of-mind. Even things said when we were young. Perhaps that's why a lot of people think they're not deserving.*

*Most people don't grow up hearing, "You can accomplish what you truly desire."*

*What do we hear instead? "Who are you kidding? You'll never be a …" "Money doesn't grow on trees. You have to earn your keep." That's more the phraseology, at least for my generation. When you hear messages like that over and over again, they do have an influence.*

*And that can become the language you think in.*

Do you think most people's intrapersonal dialogue is more negative or more positive? Or can you put a polarization on it?

*I'm not sure you can generalize like that, but it's fair to say most people don't think about their internal dialogue or manage it. It's so automatic that they become used to it.*

*It's possible to learn how to manage that internal dialogue, however.*

*At NADIA Communications, we always say, "Communication isn't just sending a message; it's creating understanding, clearly and precisely." Just because you can talk doesn't mean you are communicating. Talking can be automatic.*

*Our internal dialogue can also be automatic. We need to remember we are communicating with ourselves.*

*When you were playing football, did you have any negative dialogue going on in your head?*

Sure. I would call myself a jerk from time to time, and I could build up my opponent so that he could seem much bigger than he was. Mentally, I would sometimes think I was going against somebody that can't be blocked. I could also do the same thing and take that opponent down by making him seem much smaller than he was. I could build them up or tear them down.

I also had internal dialogue about myself. There were times when I went to a line of scrimmage with internal dialogue that I could not be beat. I was not going to counteract them. And I actually felt bigger than I was, like I took up more space and was stronger.

*That was powerful internal dialogue.*

A similar situation occurred that I'll never forget. When we went down to play the Washington Redskins at RFK Stadium, every time they scored, they'd shoot off this stupid cannon and they would sing, "Hail to the Redskins." I can still hear the tune in my head! It was this theme song that would get inside your head, and, as a Dallas Cowboy, you'd be singing "Hail to the Redskins" in your head! It just seeped in there.

*We all know that certain songs and advertising jingles anchor immediate thought. Just like there are sayings and looks that bring on a*

*particular reaction, there are certain cues for information that can come up in our minds and make us feel secure or insecure, happy or sad. These anchors create association. It's critical to be aware of the language we think in.*

How does that internal language get there in the first place?

*The same way regular language gets there. We learn our language by modeling. We watch other people, listen to other people, and that's how we pick up language. Those messages seep into our heads and stay with us.*

*Sometimes when a situation is emotionally intense, internal dialogue becomes an imprint. When people go through a very traumatic experience, maybe life threatening, they actually form reticular pathways, so their reaction is imbedded in their brains. They can relive it photographically. They hear words actually as they were spoken. It's similar to how veterans might respond to certain sounds, like a car backfiring. That sound can bring back a whole scene that was horrifying.*

*When you're a little kid, if someone is always screaming and yelling at you, that can become part of your reaction language.*

Just the way certain sounds and tones capture your attention when you're listening to someone speak, the same thing happens inside your head.

*You're right. We also have sounds and tones when we speak to ourselves. "You're a JOKE." I heard it the same way it was originally said.*

That negative emphasis is right there, isn't it?

*Sometimes our internal dialogue can have especially negative tones, not necessarily negative words. Here's one that people have told me they hear: "WHO...do you...THINK you ARE?!" It's not simply, "Who do you think you are?" There is more emphasis on the words "who" and "think" and "are." And there are strong pauses after the "who" and the first "you." That turns the whole question into something that sounds destructive.*

*We actually hear, not just words, but sounds and tones in our heads. When people say things to us that have negative tones, we want to back away from them. And yet, we do that to ourselves.*

Do you think one reason why headphones became so popular is that they prevent us from

hearing that language inside our heads? We just cover our ears and concentrate on something else.

*That's an interesting thought.*

Sometimes the internal dialogue is so strong you don't even hear the music. You just can't get rid of that one pulsating thought.

*But we do have a choice. Just as we have the choice to study French, German, Japanese, or any other language, we certainly can change the language we think in.*

We can create a new Berlitz™ in our mind.

*We can do something to retrain ourselves. When we hear a phrase like "You're a joke," we can edit it out completely or substitute something else in its place. We can listen to ourselves. We can become our own audience.*

*There are times when it's good to have a little negative thought; for instance, when we've done something that's not appropriate. It's good for our conscious self to say, "That wasn't a good thing to do," or to have some kind of a monitoring device.*

*Generally, however, our negative internal dialogue doesn't help us out.*

*In the same way we write down our words and edit them, we also have the power to edit them in our minds so that they are reframed when we speak. Just like you hear what I'm saying, I hear what I'm saying. So I have to remember that I'm getting feedback from my own messages.*

*There's so much internal dialogue going on in our minds. We need to monitor it all the time.*

*Reframing what we say to ourselves is a skill we can learn. Once we learn to reframe, we have to continue to use it, to give ourselves B12 shots when we need them. It's so easy to forget that we have the power to change our internal dialogue. At the end of the day, what's your internal dialogue? How about when you get up in the morning? Before you speak to anyone else, do you say "Great day"? What messages are you delivering in your intrapersonal circuit as you open and close your own day?*

Internal messages can really make or break our day.

*That's right. We know that our power is in the*

*present. That's the only part of our lives we can control. That means when I have a thought, I also have the power to change my thought and, therefore, change my present.*

In our work with people in public speaking, we know it's possible for people to change ineffective language patterns. They can gradually remove bad habits so they speak with more flow, deliver clear and concise messages and create understanding. We even help them to remove their "ums," their "uhs," and "you knows," and any other language that's distracting.

*People can do the same thing with their internal language.*

I recall saying to you years ago, "I hope one day I can work at Fox…" and you reframed it to "When I work at Fox…" You were doing for me externally what I could learn to do for myself internally.

*A few years ago, I went to Chicago to take care of my sister after she was released from the hospital. She had literally collapsed from exhaustion. So I asked her, "Why do you drive yourself so hard?" All she could do at that point was cry.*

12

*She was upstairs resting. I brought her some soup and she said, "I'm so lazy." In amazement, I responded, "You're so lazy? I want you to think about what you said and here's what I want you to say instead, 'I'm resting so my body can get strong again.'" That's a very different thought.*

*When I asked her where that thought came from that "she was lazy," she gave three or four examples. It was clear to me that her internal dialogue was part of the reason she was driving herself so hard. I explained that she could change that. It's okay when you've just come out of the hospital to rest! You don't have to jump up and start working.*

I'm sure a lot of people can relate to that.

*When you were an offensive lineman playing football, did you ever have to have mad, awful, angry thoughts that you repeated all the time so that you could hit a person? Wasn't that your job — to hit somebody? It seems logical that you would have to find a reason to do that.*

You do. You have to create anger. Yes, that's what you have to do. It's really sadistic. In fact, it was hard to turn it off.

*So you managed your internal messages. If we go back to our position that the power is in the moment, you're a perfect example of that. You were able to create internal dialogue that manifested anger so that you could do what you needed to do in that present moment.*

That's what I did.

*In the career you're in now, your power in the moment is with messages that say, "I want to have flow. I don't want confrontation. I want to enjoy announcing the game. I want to enjoy the relationship I have with my partner who announces with me." You're a perfect example of managing your internal dialogue.*

*In the corporate world, when a company is really culturally aligned, they think about their product, and they think about their goals. That becomes the language they "think" in. Not just what they say out loud, but it's internalized. Especially when it's a very simple message, leaders can create a culture of success in a company.*

*Sometimes companies realize they need to re-language a statement. For example, one of my technology clients had a term "talent acquisition." When I first heard it, I had this image of people tap dancing! They decided to re-language that statement to emphasize people development and talent recruitment.*

That kind of change could make a big difference.

*Changing the language we think in is not an instantaneous thing, but a process.*

*A friend of mine whose husband died when she was only 39 years old had to re-language her thoughts to be able to move ahead with her life. She and her husband had a wonderful relationship, and she was left alone with three children.*

*I really admire the way she was able to be grateful for the relationship she had with Tom. She learned a lot from it, and he will always be a piece of her life and her children's lives. She had to re-language to be able to recognize that part of her life was over. She has committed herself to a full life again, and the re-languaging she has done in her mind appears on her lips and in her life.*

When somebody recognizes that they want to change their intrapersonal dialogue, what should they do?

*I recommend two immediate actions: Ask yourself, "Where did that message come from?" Then, either delete it or reframe the message to make it more positive and constructive.*

# Pure Intent

It all began with pure intent. The vision became clear. Administrative support staff at AlliedSignal needed new skills and tools to further enable their contributions and add greater value to the company by developing their potential. Be the Best! was the outcome of that vision.

Nadine Ellerthorpe
Founding Team Member,
"Be the Best"
AlliedSignal (1991)

*Pure intent is simple. You don't think about an angle. You just act from what's pure and honest. Pure intent is your True North.*

*Nadine Udall Fischer*

17

# Pure Intent

*I initially used the phrase "pure intent" to help leaders deliver powerful messages. Pure intent is when the thought – the reason behind something – is absolutely focused and pure. Business leaders who are operating from a mindset of pure intent ask themselves a key question every time they make a decision, "Is this really the best decision for the business, not just for me personally?"*

When I think of somebody speaking with pure intent, it's almost like you can look inside them, and you can see a hidden piece of sunshine in there, like a real energy source.

It's like cutting into a Sunday morning donut. It's Boston cream inside. Just pure. You know exactly what's inside it. That's all it is.

*When a leadership team is truly functional, the leaders have the goals of the overall business in mind. That supersedes their individual territorialism, their individual concerns. It supersedes attitudes of "I want recognition" or, "I want to be the one who says the most or interrupts most." It supersedes ego.*

*Dysfunctional leadership teams — and I've*

*worked with a few of those — have individual or selfish interests, rather than the pure intent for the success of the whole business.*

*A symphony orchestra is actually a good example of a team functioning with pure intent. The conductor leads the orchestra, but every instrument, every musician, needs to play their best when it's their time. However, if someone decided, "I want to be the loudest instrument here," it would ruin the effect. There would be dissonance rather than harmony.*

*Once in a while someone in the orchestra has a solo, then that soloist stops and becomes part of the symphony again. As long as there's pure intent from all the musicians, the orchestra produces an outstanding performance.*

All the individuals are contributing to the whole unit with one purpose.

*When the conductor has pure intent, he has the power to align an entire orchestra.*

*I've talked to a lot of corporate leaders about pure intent. It's a good fit for business. People motivated by pure intent see themselves as serving a larger purpose. Part of pure intent is doing the right things for the right reasons.*

*People who operate from pure intent enjoy see-*
*ing others succeed, and they're not intimidated*
*or jealous of someone else's success. I had the*
*privilege recently of working with a senior ex-*
*ecutive who absolutely wants people to suc-*
*ceed. I observed this in his organization, and I*
*experienced it firsthand. While I was coaching*
*him on communication skills, he wanted to*
*coach me on business skills!*

*I'm sure this quality is going to be an impor-*
*tant one for him now as he moves into a CEO*
*position.*

Personally, when I started applying pure intent
to my career transition, I had to follow what
was inside of me. There was no book to read on
how to become a broadcaster. There was no
blueprint out there to follow.

In almost everything that I do, whether it's
hosting a television show or finding out information about a team, all I think about is being
the best broadcaster I can be. If a coach feels
like I'm infringing on his team practice, or I'm
asking difficult questions, it's all within the
framework of delivering the best broadcast
possible.

When I work with people, I think they can feel

that I have pure intent. There's no attack being made. There's no interest in delivering dirt, or sensationalizing some incident that occurred.

Pure intent is an energy people can feel.

*I agree. In many companies where I've worked, people say they have to be concerned about the political system. To me, that immediately takes away pure intent. If you're thinking about "what do I have to do to get ahead," not "how do I do this project well," how can there possibly be pure intent?*

*When the political hard-wiring is so thick, it's a minefield, and it's difficult to have pure and focused energy.*

*Dr. Loy McGinnis, in his book,* Bringing out the Best in People, *talks about two different kinds of communication: manipulative communication, where the communication is for me, and motivational communication, where you really have the best interest of the other person (or business) at heart.*

*People who have pure intent believe in inclusion versus exclusion. If someone within the organization can add value, they want that person to be a part of the team, to come on in and help. They genuinely care about people at every level of the organization, and they trust others to get things done.*

*When one of the big fast food companies decided they wanted to "eat" part of a competitor's market share, every Thursday they delivered a motivational and updated voice mail message to literally everyone in the organization. They involved everyone in the goal, and they succeeded.*

*Another company I'm working with right now is using a similar technique. To make sure everyone hears the voice of leadership, they are using voice mail and face-to-face communication to convey simple, important messages about the company's business strategy. They could use email, but they have chosen not to because they know that tone of voice and physical presence adds so much impact to a message.*

*Having pure intent means you commit the time, the energy and the resources, to something you believe will make a positive difference in the business. You're also courageous enough to take unpleasant action when you absolutely need to.*

*One of the things we talk about in our seminars is powerless versus powerful language. People who use powerless language identify a problem, then they take steps back. They literally move backwards. They surround themselves with a support group, and they whine and moan and complain about the problem. They never get anything done about it.*

*With powerful language, somebody identifies a problem and rather than retreat, they move forward and they engage with the people they need to in order to help find a solution to that problem. They're not afraid to face it. Their pure intent, their desired outcome, is to create a solution, not just complain.*

*Powerless language retreats. Powerful language identifies, engages, and moves forward. It has pure intent. It wants a solution.*

*Nadine Ellerthorpe led a team to bring a new vision to light at AlliedSignal.*

It all began with pure intent. It was the early 90s and the business world was changing rapidly due to globalization and more sophisticated technologies. Organizations were becoming flatter as functional and admin areas were being trimmed to operate as leanly as possible. Secretaries (now more officially called administrative assistants) were being asked to play a greater role.

The vision became clear and the intent pure. Administrative support staff needed new skills and tools to further enable their contributions and add greater value to their functions by developing their potential. Be the Best! was the outcome of that vision. A training and development program geared toward the admin/functional support staff. The program was so well received that it actually became available to anyone with the desire to better their skills and tools.

A small team embraced that vision and made it reality. When first launched, Be the Best! began with about ten training programs beginning with a personal assessment and including programs in several arenas: business acumen, leadership, interpersonal skills, and technical skills. Skill building classes like Teambuilding, Effective Communication, Engaged Listening, Creative Thinking, etc. The program took off. AlliedSignal was at the cutting edge of developing and recognizing the hidden talent within the administrative function.

Be the Best! remained evergreen. Each year, the programs were evaluated, upgraded, and expanded as the bar was raised even higher. The pure intent led to even greater aspirations for this population as a large percent then began working toward their undergraduate degrees, and a few are currently working toward their Master's or some personal level of higher education.

*A great example of how opening one door leads to so many choices, inspires, and motivates...and it all began with pure intent.*

Pure intent is simple.

*Because you don't have to think about the angle. You don't have to cover yourself. You just act from what's honest and pure.*

If you look at companies that have sprung up from the beginning of time, whether it was during the industrial revolution or whatever era, the ones that survived were the ones who recognized a need. Pure intent cut through everything.

Pure intent is like a laser. A person can have a self-generated laser. It starts with that sunshine inside you and the radiation of light is really a direct line.

*And it moves forward, like powerful language. It moves forward and engages where it needs to engage, without damaging.*

Look at a man like Gandhi. He was a very average, nondescript Indian who thought it was time for independence. He knew somebody had to make a stand for independence because he believed the country should no longer be under colonial rule. Isn't it fascinating that one man could galvanize a nation? That's how powerful pure intent is.

We're talking about a really powerful source here — in everything.

When I had the goal of becoming a broadcaster, I wanted to do the things I needed to do for the right reason. I can look back now and say that every single step was necessary and important. And I gave the very best I could give.

I honestly feel that I was rewarded with the position I have now because all of my actions were for the right reason.

*Because you had pure intent.*

*Thinking about pure intent makes decisions easier for everybody.*

*In a leadership meeting, a company may decide they want to have 34% of their growth in a certain global market. If that's truly a goal, but another leader on the team has a vested interest in another market, then they may not be able to achieve that desired outcome.*

*It starts on a personal level. The individual has to be aligned with the desired outcomes. And then it moves ahead. Pure intent can occur with a two-person team like you and me, or it can happen with twelve people on a leadership team.*

Or, with eleven people on a football team.

*If we have pure intent, it is our True North. We always come back to it so that we will accomplish our desired outcomes.*

It's like Polaris, the North Star. For centuries, it was the focal point for travelers to navigate through difficult passages. There was no global positioning system then!

Pure intent really does apply to our personal lives, our personal navigation system.

*If we pay attention to it, yes.*

Who are some business people who have pure intent?

*Lynn Brown, a corporate executive, recently identified several CEOs and "thought leaders" who exhibit qualities of pure intent. She selected Fred Poses, CEO at American Standard;*

*Jamie Houghton, CEO at Corning; Warren Wilhelm, President of Global Consulting Alliance; Dennis Malimatinus, former CEO at Burger King; David Ulrich of the University of Michigan; and Larry Bossidy, former CEO at AlliedSignal/Honeywell.*

What makes them pure intent "winners"?

*When she and I were discussing this concept, she came up with suggestions that I think hit the mark in describing common characteristics of people with pure intent.*

*This list puts it in a very simple, clear format. It's a map to pure intent!*

*People who have pure intent:*

- *Can see the big picture and possess the ability to execute.*
- *Genuinely care about people at every level of the organization they serve and believe in inclusion.*
- *Trust others to get things done.*
- *Are good, quick judges of character.*
- *Are willing to be open, direct, and honest.*
- *Know how to influence and persuade others to get on board.*

- *Enjoy seeing others succeed and reward the good work that people do.*
- *Are easily identified as a leader by their organization.*
- *Are tough and courageous enough to take unpleasant action and appropriate risks when they need to.*
- *Are not stopped by the discomfort or criticism of others and do not take the convenient or easy way out if it is the wrong choice.*
- *Have high standards and insist on a certain level of quality.*
- *Are experts in their fields of work.*

# The Four Factors

Our mission is to offer world-class health solutions to our customers, taking the best of the old and the most innovative of the new. We could not possibly accomplish that without understanding four factors: history, environment, context, and the present.

Strategy is not about trying to figure out how to climb the mountain. It is about clearly understanding which mountain to climb.

> Dr. Bob Lufrano
> President
> BlueCross BlueShield Florida

*The four factors have great influence over any communication situation or strategy. Ask yourself these questions:*

- *Have I researched the history?*
- *What kind of environment do I want to create?*
- *What's the context that surrounds this situation?*
- *Am I 100% present right here, right now?*

> *Nadine Udall Fischer*

# The Four Factors

*In my coaching work with executives, I wanted to give people a formula to help them analyze situations in order to communicate a clear message. As I thought categorically, I came up with four factors: history, environment, context, and the present.*

*These four factors always have great influence over any communication situation or strategy. They apply whether I'm coaching someone who is going to give a presentation or whether I'm working with a leadership team to help them develop and communicate a business strategy.*

I know what you mean. I'm often asked to give a motivational speech about my experiences as a professional football player. That's fine. I'm comfortable with that. But if I'm going to a juvenile detention center to talk with kids who have been in trouble, my usual presentation isn't going to work.

I have to change it to talk to them on a more visceral level. It needs to be audience-appropriate. I have to understand their history. These kids have never been given the opportunities I've had, and they've rarely been told

anything good about themselves. Whatever I say, it has to fit them.

It seems to me that the most powerful of the four factors is history. Am I right on that?

*Absolutely. Because you and I are a composite.*

*Look at language. Where does language come from? Language is a modeled behavior. From the time we are babies we start to learn certain sounds, phrases, and sentences.*

*Inside every human being is a software program.*

Not only every human being but every organization, team, family, and even schools, have a unique history.

*I had an experience in high school that changed the course of my history. When I was 16, I went to my guidance counselor and told her that I wanted to go to college and study speech. She responded in a haughty, pompous voice that I will never forget. She said, "Nadine, you will 'nevah' get into one of the 'bettah' schools." Those were her exact words.*

*I left her office with such pain in my throat. It*

*felt as though I had a space the size of a pea left to breathe. All I wanted to do was cry.*

*I then took the public bus home — we didn't have school buses that went to my outlying sending district. I had about 45 minutes to see my father because he worked two jobs. He climbed telephone poles from eight in the morning till five, and then he worked at a gas station pumping gas from six until ten at night to support our family.*

*When my father saw me, he realized right away that something was wrong. He was great at picking up visual language. As soon as he said, "What's wrong?" the tears came and in a trembling voice, I told him, "My guidance counselor said I can never get into college and I want to go to college." He said, "I'll go and talk with her."*

*Now I wish I could say I was thrilled, but I wasn't. My father had never gone to school with me — ever. That wasn't his thing.*

*And so, on the appointed day, he went down to the basement and washed his hands with Borax and Lava soap, and we went to see the guidance counselor. When we walked into her office, he said to her, "Sit down." And she did.*

*What an amazing piece of language that was.*

*The outcome of that day was an undergraduate degree earned on a total scholarship. Perhaps I went to a college my guidance counselor didn't think was one of the "bettah" schools, but at Montclair State, now Montclair University, I received one of the best educations possible with professors who cared, in a small speech department with a strong program in communications. That experience made all the difference in my life. Those professors brought out talents and gifts I never even knew I had.*

*Language changes lives.*

*I always challenge the people I work with to pay attention to what they say to other people because we have the power to change people's lives. And, unfortunately, not always for the better.*

*Thinking about the impact of history when I'm coaching people, I often wonder what their defining moments have been.*

In the sports world, knowing about history is vital.

When Bill Parcells went to the New York Jets, they hadn't won in about 15 years. They had great fans, but when anything started to go bad in a game, people just thought, "Here go the Jets. They play hard, but we knew they would lose."

*That mindset almost makes it seem like losing is okay. Losing is their history. Not only are they set up to fail, they anticipate failing, they expect to fail. When the expectations are so low, how do you raise the expectations?*

Bill Parcells went to the Jets knowing their history. The first thing he did was change their uniforms. He changed the logo back to when they were winners. Parcells changed the visual right away, which I thought was pretty smart. A lot of former coaches knew the Jets' history, but none of those coaches had made that change.

Bill Parcells went in with the attitude of, "How do we use their history in our favor?" He returned the Jets psychologically to the time when they won the Super Bowl with Joe Namath 30 years ago. They went back to the time when they were winners, and it helped them improve their performance.

*Sometimes just understanding the history is enough to make a big difference in your actions.*

*Environment, the next of the four factors, can be a valuable addition to analyzing history, or it can be worthwhile just to analyze it alone. In the world of television, I'll bet environment has a big impact on you.*

No doubt about it. In the television business, if you're in a cold, sterile studio, and you have to deliver an energetic piece of information, it's a difficult atmosphere. Whereas, if you're on the set of David Letterman, you've got 500 people cheering for you. You're able to feed off their energy. It's a very different environment.

One of the things that makes Terry Bradshaw so great is that he can do a pre-game show in a very sterile environment and still act enthused. They're in there at five in the morning, and the set is dingy and it's dark, and then the lights come on and it's show time for Terry.

It's interesting that four or five times a year, they'll take that pre-game show and put it on the road. They set up their booth right in the stadium, and the ratings are always higher. The energy is so much greater when they are in a live place, like at the Super Bowl, or at Lambeau Field in Green Bay, or if they're in Texas Stadium. There's a difference just because the environment is different.

*Think about how people feel when they walk into a hospital, when they get near an operating room. That environment has a definite impact on most of us.*

When I went to Duke, I was enrolled in the pre-medical program. I lived in an off-campus apartment and a short cut to the campus was through the hospital. You could literally cut through the hospital and come out on campus. You'd save yourself about a ten-minute walk.

Walking through that environment every day for three years became a bit depressing for me, and so I changed my career plans.

*Some hospitals, because of the change in healthcare, have realized they have to change their environment.*

What have they done?

*They work on being more friendly, even open, bright, and airy.*

You mean the physical structure?

*Yes. Even the color of the walls and the furniture. The physical environment changes the perception people have.*

*Environment, of course, isn't limited to places, like hospitals or stadiums. Just think about what the industrial revolution did to the environment. No one gave any thought to what the long-term negative effect could be. Everybody just surged ahead. We weren't prepared for the pollution it created, and we've had to spend decades cleaning up. Today we're in the age of information, and now we're polluting the human system because it wasn't hard-wired for the amount and kinds of information that we're getting.*

I was thinking about that hard-wired idea last night when I was in the ESPN studio. There's no way we were hard-wired to sit in a room with 14 different television screens all giving us information and being able to absorb that. It's very uncomfortable sitting there. It's just non-stop noise. You're exhausted when you leave.

*Do you still turn the radio off when you drive to a game?*

Yes. That's something I've done to give myself some peace and quiet and sort through my thoughts as I get ready for a game. I like music, but it's everywhere you go. The gym has music, elevators have music. I don't have to have music when I drive. I like the solitude.

*It's great that you've recognized that. We all have the power to create our own environment. We can carve out some time for peace and quiet if we want to.*

*In David Shenk's book,* Data Smog, *he talks about Attention Deficit Disorder — ADD — as an epidemic. We have cultural ADD. People are extremely restless and they have difficulty concentrating on anything for more than a few moments. The cause is simply an overload of information.*

*At times, information becomes a pollutant.*

*Human beings are as polluted from information as our environment was. There were rivers we couldn't swim in and oceans that were dangerous because we just dumped stuff. Now we are dumping information. We have to be discerning to think about what we really need. As human beings, we have choices to make every day. We have some control over our environment.*

Context, however, is one of the four factors we can't always control. I've heard you say context is what surrounds any situation we're walking into. I had an interesting experience where the context had a tremendous impact on my presentation. I was speaking at a local chapter of football officials. These were high school, college, and professional football officials. I had prepared a particular speech about my own personal experiences as a player and a broadcaster.

Well, I arrived a little bit late because of bad weather. There was an open bar and these officials had had a little too much time at the bar. They were far too loose for my prepared comments. They wanted locker room stories. So, I loosened my tie and joined the festive atmosphere.

*You did a quick analysis of the context and made the right decision, I'm sure.*

*Context does not always show up on the surface. It sometimes requires a bit of investigation or research. Think about the expression teachers often use when they help their students understand new vocabulary. They encourage the student to figure it out from the context. Leaders may have to do the same kind of investigative work.*

The last of the four factors is the present. How does the present fit into the whole picture?

*My theory about the present is that you need to be 100% here right now — intellectually, physically, emotionally. The power is in the present moment. The power is not in the past, it's not in tomorrow.*

Why?

*Because today is where all our human energy is at this moment in time. Any change I want to make in my life, any difference I want to make, can only be done in the present.*

*Very few people that I meet really live in the present moment. They are so often in internal dialogue thinking about what happened before and why they feel badly about it, or what bothers them. That saps their energy. Or, they're thinking about what they need to do tomorrow, what's on their desks, all of their obligations, and that saps their energy. When we think about doing something, it literally drains our energy. It's just like doing it physically.*

*When we learn to live in the present, we under-stand that the power is right here, right now. Unfortunately, we often let some things inter-fere.*

It happens all the time in the sports world.

Here's the classic situation. A team has a game to play on Sunday, but they're playing their ul-timate rival the following Sunday at home. Everybody is talking about that rival game at home next week and how big it is on the sched-ule, but there's a game to play this weekend. Everybody's overlooking this game. The me-dia's overlooking it. The players are talking about next week's game, they're anticipating the turnout and the families and friends that are coming, what happened last year, and revenge, or whatever. And they're not thinking about this present game.

Their energy isn't here on this day, on the game they should win or are supposed to win. They end up losing because they're not focused. It's a classic case in sports. It happens every single Sunday.

*In the corporate world people are so over-meetinged. I see a lot of individuals who are really not in the meeting at all. Their minds are somewhere else. One of the greatest qualities of the best leaders is emotional sovereignty, being able to create that wall so that emotional "bleed" from another situation doesn't leak through, so you can be present, emotionally and intellectually. Right here, right now.*

*If we have an unpleasant meeting or a problem, that can carry through to another experience. Think about customer contact. Let's say someone has a very negative customer experience and they carry that over to the next customer encounter. Instead of that new customer getting a fresh human being, they get the leftovers!*

*Learning how to be fully alive in this moment is one of the hardest things to do and one of the greatest opportunities we have.*

*Here's what happens if I'm having a conversation with you, but am in internal dialogue about an employee whose performance is poor. I physically can't hear you. What you're saying becomes just masking noise to me, just white noise or background noise. We're not connecting, we're not in the present, we're not engaged with one another.*

In the broadcasting business, we spend a week to prepare for the game on Sunday. You plan all

week and you try to predict how the game will go. But the game may go in a completely different direction.

Everything you may have been planning, you have to be ready to let it go. You have to be ready to talk about what's happening right now, not what you thought was going to happen on Wednesday or Thursday. Otherwise, the broadcast will sound very forced; it's not going to flow.

*That's why the present is so important. Didn't you tell me you found a new way to approach your broadcasts where you're focusing more on the present?*

I used to feel like I was being bombarded with way too much information in preparing for each week's game. I wanted to simplify it. So I thought, "What if I do all my normal preparation, and then leave all my notes at home and go in there with nothing but a map, just rely on my own memory map, not think about all the other notes? Whatever the game dictates is what I'll commentate on." What I found was that I actually could have conversations with people without thinking, "Oh, what did that guy say in that interview last week?"

I stopped worrying and thinking about all those things I had read. I went to the game just like a fan — completely relaxed. I didn't have the headache you get when you're trying to remember too much stuff. At the end of the game, I didn't feel drained or tired.

During a sports broadcast I have to deliver what's called an "open." That's the time to let the audience know why they should watch this game, who to look for, and what the theme is going to be. I used to try to memorize exactly what I wanted to say, even down to the syntax and the adjectives. The results were that I was mistake-free, but it didn't seem natural or authentic.

What I needed to do was just listen to my partner's question and react and respond naturally, like I would at any other time.

*It's like giving a speech. You need to be prepared and know your material. Standing in front of a group unless you "know your stuff" can be dangerous. When you begin your speech, as long as you have done your homework and your message is mapped, you can move into a place called flow. That's where you're in the present moment and on top of*

*your material. You haven't memorized the presentation word for word. You're delivering in the present moment. That's the best way to deliver a speech.*

A few years ago, I watched John Madden and Pat Summerall, the number one broadcast team in all of sports, with no sound but close-captioned. I was actually just reading the words that John Madden was saying. Do you know how simple his language is? I guess what makes him a success is his timing. It's the *way* that he says it. It's the control he has and the spirit he has. He's absolutely in the present.

*If you go back to the study done by Dr. Albert Mehrabian at U.C.L.A., we know that our words play a small part in influencing people. Our non-verbals are worth 55%, sounds and tones are 38%, and the actual words, what you read on that TV screen, are only 7%. What you've just explained says those percentages are pretty accurate.*

Most people who don't communicate effectively think what they have to say is way more important than how they say it or how it sounds.

*We're not talking about not preparing. You need to know the content and be an expert. Those Mehrabian statistics are about what happens at the absolute moment of delivery.*

We've talked a lot about the four factors, but we need a concrete method to use when we analyze a situation.

*I like to work with questions. As I mentioned in the opening to this chapter, here are key questions we can ask ourselves or share with others:*

- *Have I researched the history?*

- *What kind of environment do I want to create?*

- *What's the context that surrounds this situation?*

- *Am I 100% present right here, right now? What do I need to change if I'm not totally present?*

# Message Mapping

Message Mapping accomplishes three objectives for you. First, it organizes your thoughts in a logical fashion so that you know the messages or "the story" that you want to communicate. Second, the audience understands the message significantly faster because you have made it easy for them. Finally, you will be far more relaxed and confident in your delivery because you know you will be understood.

Whether I am preparing a presentation for a ballroom audience or collecting my thoughts to speak extemporaneously to a small group, Message Mapping is a winning formula. It is a great technique to improve your communication skills.

Matt Farrell
C.F.O.
Alpharma

*The visual framework of a Message Map helps people focus on critical messages, use a logical structure, and chunk information.*

*It keeps communicators on track.*

*Nadine Udall Fischer*

# Message Mapping

One of the best techniques I learned from you was how to use Message Mapping. It helps so much when I prepare for a presentation, to make a vertical map of my introduction, three or four key messages, and then my close. All I have to do after that is organize my stories or examples.

*I created Message Mapping so that people would have a visual model in their minds. We frequently think visually because we've become such a media-literate society.*

*It's so easy to see the main points in vertical boxes and the supporting information on horizontal lines. Since a Message Map forces people to chunk information, it keeps communicators on track.*

*So often, executives are asked to speak extemporaneously. "Can you come into this meeting and speak for five minutes?" Executives I work with begin to think in a Message Mapping style. The template is in their brain.*

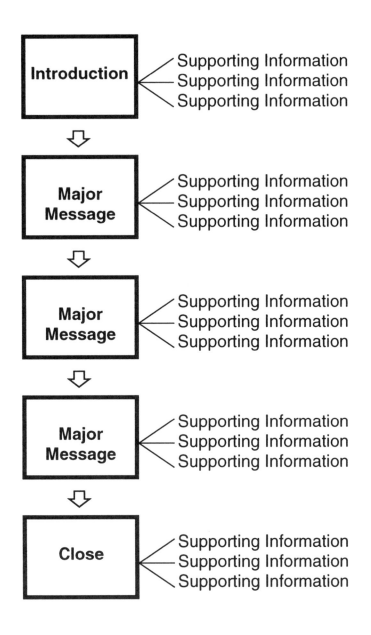

Introduction — Supporting Information / Supporting Information / Supporting Information

Major Message — Supporting Information / Supporting Information / Supporting Information

Major Message — Supporting Information / Supporting Information / Supporting Information

Major Message — Supporting Information / Supporting Information / Supporting Information

Close — Supporting Information / Supporting Information / Supporting Information

*Some people use a Message Map template on their laptops, others use it on paper, but eventually everyone who uses it begins to think about their message in specific questions: What are my desired outcomes? What are my top three or four key ideas? How can I support those ideas with anecdotes, data, whatever?*

*The Message Map really becomes the architecture. If we were going to build a house, we would make sure that, first of all, we decided what style it's going to be. We'd get the architectural plan together, and then we'd begin to build. The last thing we would do is paint and wallpaper the walls.*

*I've noted in the corporate world that the first thing people do is create their visuals — their slides, overheads, or their PowerPoint presentation. They create 60 or 70 or 80 of them, and then they re-create them, and then they re-create them again! They invest so much time in the visuals rather than starting with the architecture of the message.*

*The Message Map forces people to have an architectural plan for their presentation. Once they have decided on three or four key*

*ideas, they focus on the ancillaries, the anecdotes and the visuals that enhance their key ideas.*

*The power of the presentation should be on the presenter, and the visual should only enhance it.*

I recall how the commissioner of the World Boxing Union was uncomfortable speaking in front of a group. You and I were sitting in his office in Miami when he told us, "When I start speaking, the audience changes the channel. They tune me out."

So you went back to his history. You got him to tell us a story. When he was 10 years old, his dad took him to Madison Square Garden to see his first boxing match. When he felt the electricity of the match, he got hooked on boxing. As he was telling us this, you and I felt his excitement. That story turned out to be a great way to start his speech. He was able to grab the attention of the whole audience.

*We gave him a very simple map, and that story was one of the key pieces of it.*

As a result, he harnessed his own energy to connect with the audience.

*The visual framework of a map helps people focus on critical messages, use a logical structure, and chunk information.*

*Research shows that human beings enhance their ability to encode information by using units of threes and fours. That's why our telephone numbers and social security numbers and other lists are divided that way. This visual framework forces us to use that formula, that equation, in order to chunk our information. The Message Mapping technique helps someone stay on focus.*

*It's a very basic formula. But since great communication is making complex simple, not simple complex, it helps people sort out information, especially in our over-informationed society.*

I've found that I've started thinking vertically and horizontally. When I'm actually delivering a message, I know when I'm speaking vertically — emphasizing my key ideas — and when I'm speaking horizontally —

providing supporting facts and examples. There's a real good picture in my head.

For example, in broadcasting, if I'm going to do the Philadelphia Eagles and the Arizona Cardinals in a football game, I may take three areas of emphasis that I'm going to expose during the game. Those would be my vertical cells, and then I use shining examples to support each of those cells.

*In the Ravens vs. Giants game you did yesterday in Baltimore, what were the three or four key things you focused on?*

Since it was the last pre-season game and it was at high noon on a Friday, and most of these professional athletes hadn't played at high noon on a Friday since high school, there was a lot of concern on both sides about the intensity of the game. So, intensity of the game was the first key idea — the first box — on my Message Map.

It just so happens that when the intensity fails in a pre-season game, people get injured. They're not as alert, they're not as aware, so the coaches were really concerned that the intensity wasn't going to be there.

This was essentially a meaningless game; the decisions about most of the players had already been made. This was one of those games you just want to get over with!

We wanted to focus on the five or six players on each team that were on what is known as the bubble. A good performance in this game probably allows them to make the team. An unimpressive performance probably keeps them from making the team. There were five or six guys on each team who were fighting for their NFL lives.

The final roster was going to be set two days later. Since the teams had to go from 65 players to 53, 12 players had to be cut.

Looking at my Message Map, the first key idea was the intensity, second was the bubble players, and third was the competition at certain positions for both sides.

The fourth key idea was how important it was for the Ravens to win. They've had a losing streak for the last three years, and their coach was trying to turn attitudes around. Every win goes a little bit further in reinforcing the good feeling you get from winning.

*Who won?*

The Ravens won on the last play of the game, through a touchdown pass.

*Was it a good game?*

Yes. It was actually an exciting game. Everybody got treated to some big plays.

*So you actually Message Mapped the four areas you would focus on and all your ancillaries, your horizontals, would be stories and anecdotes to bring those points to life.*

That's right. Here's a picture of it.

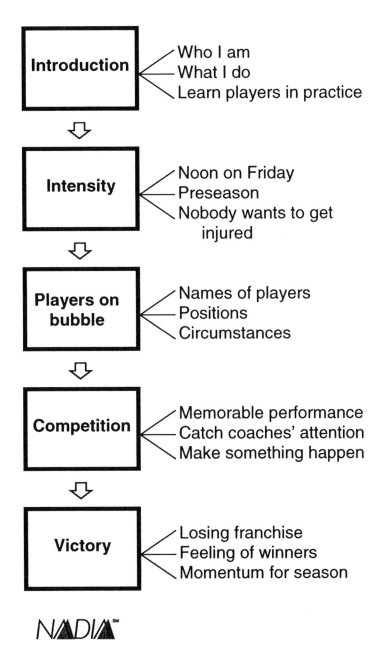

| Introduction | Who I am<br>What I do<br>Learn players in practice |

| Intensity | Noon on Friday<br>Preseason<br>Nobody wants to get<br>injured |

| Players on bubble | Names of players<br>Positions<br>Circumstances |

| Competition | Memorable performance<br>Catch coaches' attention<br>Make something happen |

| Victory | Losing franchise<br>Feeling of winners<br>Momentum for season |

NADIA℠

*Looks organized to me. Isn't it interesting that in reading someone else's Message Map, we can tell that it's organized, but, of course, we couldn't use someone else's map? It's very individual.*

When you're working with a leadership team on strategy, how do they use Message Mapping?

*Often, leadership teams, because they're extremely brilliant business people, come up with very complex strategies. We use this tool to map pieces of the strategy so that it can be clearly understood throughout the entire organization. We're doing that at a major manufacturing company right now. We may have a series of perhaps three or four maps based on large pieces of information around the strategy.*

*The president of this company finds Message Mapping to be such a useful tool that he actually insists that everybody map the information they bring to him. As a result, he can use every bit of his listening time effectively and efficiently. His entire team has learned to use this tool. He'll say, "Show me the map, and let's talk through it."*

*If you want to go from here to San Francisco but I don't tell you what route to take, and four people take different routes, we may show up at different times. But if we all are using the same map, and we're aligned, we can travel together, and we can get there in a timely manner.*

*When you think about time management, Message Mapping works really well. An executive can say, "Map it and then come in and talk me through it." Someone thinks it through first — the major issues, the desired outcomes.*

*We've had executives use Message Maps for a simple elevator speech, when they want to give a high 60,000 foot view of a business. When you're riding from the first floor to the twelfth floor and somebody asks a question about the business, the executive can quickly visualize the three or four cells on a Message Map and have the answer without stumbling.*

*At NADIA Communications we used Message Mapping to identify the key messages around our capabilities. No matter whom we meet on a plane, or someplace else, if they ask what does NADIA Communications*

*do, we all deliver a consistent message.*

*Some managers I've worked with actually create a map before they leave a voice mail to make sure they're on target and crystal clear. It's certainly a great time-saver for the person on the receiving end. But more important, that person is more likely to move ahead with the action because the message is so clear.*

*People find that Message Mapping doesn't take a lot of time and can work in impromptu situations. When you're at a dinner and someone asks you to make a few comments, do you use a map?*

Yes. I can take three minutes to map out what I'm going to say. That happens a lot.

That happened to me a couple of weeks ago in Baltimore. I drove from Philadelphia to Baltimore at six in the morning and got in there a little after eight. I was expecting to go in the cafeteria and get something to eat, read the paper, and then go to observe practice.

Well, in a room next to the cafeteria, the Baltimore Ravens' entire marketing staff was having a meeting The director of media relations stopped me in the hallway and asked me if I would address his staff right then.

I literally had just gotten out of the car, I was road-buzzed, and I hadn't eaten yet! While one other marketing guy was talking about something, I had about five minutes to think about what I was going to say. I just went into the map mode. What three things can I address here? Even if I'm not great horizontally with support because it's off the cuff, at least I'll have three clear messages to deliver.

I talked briefly about the past and the fact that they hadn't won there (in the new stadium), next about the new coach and the excitement he brought. Then, I talked about the new West Coast system with a great history of success in the NFL and what the system was going to allow this team to do this year. That's why, as a marketing group, they should be excited about working for the Ravens staff. My mental map worked!

Now that I've begun using Message Mapping, I really can apply it to every situation.

*You can see it in your mind. You visualize it.*

*Mapping is a strategic visualization and framework process. Strategic, meaning you focus on what are the key areas and desired outcomes, not all the details. It creates a clear chain of thought. It focuses on key messages and goals.*

*For that situation with the marketing staff, you wanted to motivate them. That was your desired outcome. You helped them understand why they could be excited about this team, the new coach and where the team was going.*

*Message Mapping can be used for any communication situation.*

I think people are a lot more likely to accept the challenge of going up in front of a group to say a few words when they can go with that mode and organize things a little bit better, rather than get up there and ramble.

*And we know many people that ramble!*

Way too many!

Do you ever find people who are already Message Mappers when you meet them?

*Some people have an ability to clearly think through and organize material, but this gives them an additional tool by providing a visual framework.*

*What I've noticed is that people have great difficulty organizing material because we live in such an over-informationed society. What's important? What's not important? When you get 240 emails a day, it's difficult to sort through and prioritize.*

*I mentioned the book* Data Smog *by David Shenk before. According to him, people in an office typically spend 60% of their time processing documents. Processing documents. Think about it.*

*We live in a message-dense society. To cut through that, we have to remember that memorable is not complex. Memorable is something simple enough that I can grasp it, hold on to it, remember it, and then it's useful to me.*

*The industrial revolution was a wonderful time to move us forward economically, but as I mentioned before, the clean-up required has*

*taken decades. Now we're doing the very same thing with the information revolution and the technological age, but we're doing it to the human being.*

*We have to learn how to manage this to keep from burning out. Learning to manage the information clutter in our lives is a necessity now.*

Message Mapping is a good way to work through information clutter.

*Yes. It's an extremely effective tool whether you're on a leadership team or whether you're leaving a message for the car pool about your children. It works.*

*Executives I work with who use Message Mapping, say it has helped them cut out the excessive number of visuals for a presentation. They begin to select only those visuals that enhance their message.*

*They're also better able to use visuals that have graphics or pictures to support what they're saying. Having one set of words on a screen, and another set of words coming out of someone's mouth crosses modalities. Worse* yet, somebody reading the words on the screen and calling that a presentation is truly just "reading out loud."

Most of the leaders I work with have left the everyday task world. Eighty percent to 85% of what they do is communicating.

I always ask leaders what they want to achieve. I listen and then I restate what I hear in a Message Map format. The goal is creating understanding around the desired outcomes for everyone in the organization. That clear message is the foundation for align-ment, motivation, and inspiration. That's what leaders spend most of their time doing.

I encourage leaders to remember that mis-sion constantly, whether they're on a plant floor, the hallway or in an office. Focus on the opportunities to align, motivate, and in-spire.

When we think about leadership communica-tion, the backbone of it is making complex simple so that everyone understands it. One CEO I worked with said, "At the end of the day, it's not about strategy, it's about the peo-ple that make it happen."

*Strategies live on paper. Unless they're shared and clearly understood so that people can execute them, then nobody has breathed life into that strategy.*

Nadine, do you use Message Mapping?

*Even if I'm delivering a workshop that's three or four hours, I will move through a series of maps so that everything is well organized and easy for an audience to follow. Think about my concept of the four factors: history, environment, context, and the present. Those are four vertical cells of a map. My ancillaries, whether they're visuals, anecdotes, or props enhance each one.*

I've found that Message Mapping even works in situations where you're listening to someone who is rambling. You can pull out three or four things that are important about what they're saying.

*It's true. That happens because you're listening for critical messages.*

It's like anything else that you're being coached in. If you want to excel, you put the coach inside your own head and coach yourself.

*Along with our Message Map, "Kinesthetic Power" is a great tool. Here's one of our recent "Communication Tips." Using "Kinesthetic Power" we bring our map to life.*

# Kinesthetic Power
# (What the heck is that?)

You may, or may not, find the word "kinesthetic" in your dictionary...and yet it is a word with powerful meaning. In our NADIA Communications workshops, we talk about the "modalities" that humans use to encode meaning and messages: **Visual, Auditory, Kinetic** and **KINESTHETIC**. Kinesthetic...learning through "the heart and soul."

Have you ever listened to a story that touched your heart and moved your soul? Maybe it caused you to laugh from your gut, or even brought tears to your eyes. The lesson you learned from that story leaves an imprint on you for the rest of your life. *That's* **KINESTHETIC POWER**.

For years, our NADIA Communications coaches have talked about limiting Power Point, and truly engaging with the audience. (Isn't it amazing that Abraham Lincoln's "Gettysburg Address" still lives? And he used *no* Power Point!)

Nothing can replace a great story told well, or an analogy or anecdote that enhances your key messages.

So, we were delighted when a recent Harvard Business Review article confirmed just that.

"Storytelling That Moves People" by Robert McKee and Bronwyn Fryer is an article that we highly recommend. (See bibliography.)

# Ladies and Gentlemen, Start Your Life Energy!

In today's world, strong leaders bring magnified energy and clear communication to their organizations; the very best leaders work hard to make it look easy. Nadine Fischer not only teaches you how to make communication look easy, but also makes you want to work at it.

Dave Weidman
C.O.O.
Celanese A.G.

*Life is precious. It's really about learning to live life to the fullest each and every day. It's appreciating the gift of life with every breath we take.*

*Nadine Udall Fischer*

## Ladies and Gentlemen, Start Your Life Energy!

*In the most successful companies I've worked with, the leaders have extraordinary energy. Their energy is imprinted on the entire organization.*

*A while back, I spoke with a pilot who flies for a Fortune 500 company. He told me how he enjoyed watching the CEO get off the plane simply because of the CEO's visual energy. He said he could tell that the CEO knew exactly what he was going to accomplish that day. His stance, his movement, his facial expressions - they all communicated a very clear message. (See Congruency Tip at chapter close.)*

*Often, we communicate through our visual language and our energy more clearly than we do through our words. And, people listen with their <u>eyes</u> as well as their ears!*

What affects that visual communication?

*The choices we make every day — what we think about, who we're with, how we approach challenges —they all have an impact*

*on our energy. If we're bogged down with fears and overwhelmed with stress, we have to get past those interferences to communicate most effectively and congruently.*

*Brian, do you have any tricks of the trade you use to harness your energy? How do you feel, for example, when you are asked to give an impromptu speech?*

I feel like the energy has been sapped out of me, and I have to find a way to get it back. One of the great relaxers and energy boosters for me is to talk. I talk to as many people as possible ahead of time. When I give advice to others about speaking in front of a group, I often tell them to get up and move and talk before the speech. Be as animated as you can. Don't just sit there. You get stiffer and stiffer and you're thinking all about it. Talking automatically relaxes you, gets your voice moving. I've even talked to myself out loud in my room before I go on the air.

*I often recommend j'arming — jogging with your __arms__. Dr. Dale Anderson, a medical doctor, came up with the idea of j'arming as a result of investigating why orchestra conductors live longer than the average population. (See bibliography.)*

*Typical exercise movements are lower body, but symphony conductors use their upper bodies to a great extent. Dr. Anderson came up with the idea of moving your arms just as though you're conducting an orchestra.*

*You can do j'arming anywhere. It stimulates your lungs, it increases blood circulation, it clears your mind, it helps you to breathe more deeply and it energizes you. Turn on some music and let the combination of music and j'arming get you going.*

*Many of my clients use j'arming when they have had a tough day or when their energy level is a little low. They find that j'arming gives them the boost of energy they need. A definite way to jump start your life energy!*

Anything you can do to make yourself laugh is also an energizer. Laughing automatically puts you in a good frame of mind. I used to do an opener with my former partner, Curt, and before the camera was on, I'd just look at him and start laughing. It's almost like a laugh

track. Then, when the camera came on, I was relaxed and smiling. It takes the seriousness away from the situation.

*I know a lot of people who recall moments that made them feel terrific, a moment of wonderful life energy.*

*One of my business colleagues who conducts training seminars has a great method for boosting her energy. When she was in high school, her theatre coach said to her, "Knock 'em dead!" right before she walked onstage as the leading lady in a musical. Her standard routine before every seminar is to say to herself, "Knock 'em dead!" She's been doing that for more than 20 years.*

*Our minds are incredible warehouses filled with thoughts and memories that we can call up in an instant. We can easily recall defining moments when we felt great. What's the first thing that comes to your mind when you think of feeling fantastic?*

I remember being in Dallas in the 6060 Hotel when there were 14 rookies left competing for 6 spots with the Dallas Cowboys. We were the final 14 rookies out of a hundred, and the decision was being made as I was sitting in that hotel room.

The head of personnel called and asked me, "Do you think you can make dinner tomorrow night at such and such a place?" Well, if it's tomorrow night, it's basically an invitation to join the team. So I said, "Does this mean I made the team?" He said, "Well, we're not going to invite somebody that didn't make the team!" When I hung up the phone, it was one of those times when you're glad nobody's around. You can just sit there and breathe and close your eyes and savor the moment. You don't want to jump up and down and celebrate yet. You just want to glow.

To this day, my greatest achievement in life, period, was making the Dallas Cowboys. I don't know if anything else will ever measure up to that. But to this day, that feeling of making that team against those odds and what I had to go through, to me, that was the greatest joy I've experienced in life.

What's so great about having that type of joy in life is that nobody can ever take it away. You can always call it back.

*Do you realize that without a lot of effort you just recalled a very special moment when you felt great? And I watched how you felt as you relived it.*

*We're talking about language here. We're talking about words and phrases and how those become etched into our memory banks. Those words create that feeling...in this case a great feeling.*

*Recreating experiences like these is one way to get our energy and confidence up, even for situations like speaking in front of a group.*

Sometimes people need to come into a room and be on right away, like maybe someone comes up to an executive and says, "I need you in the room to give a 10-minute pep talk." How can they flip a switch and be ready to do that instantaneously? That's tough to do. What do you do? Do you feel nervous when you speak to those groups?

*I feel something in the pit of my stomach.*

I always feel nervous.

*That's a good feeling to have because it means*

*you want to connect with your audience.
That feeling is your energy. That's your body
saying, "I want to do this right." The gift is
to be able to take that energy and make it
work for you.*

*Almost fifteen years ago, I had the dream of
publishing a book. I'd sent query letters and
received many rejections. One day another
rejection crossed my desk. The thought occurred to me to just give up. That same day,
one other piece of mail arrived. When I
opened it, a copy of an Erma Bombeck article fell out. The article was entitled "Taking
Your Dreams Out of the Box."*

*The article talked about a young woman who
wrote poetry and dreamed of having it published. Finally one day she received a check
for $5.00 because one of her poems had been
accepted. Now, $5.00 isn't a lot of money, but
self-fulfillment is priceless.*

*Bombeck went on to talk about how hard it
can be to take your dreams out of the box.
Once you take them out, people can laugh at
them, criticize and demean them. Even call
them a "joke." And so, far too often, we stuff
our dreams back in the box. Then I realized*

*there was a small note attached to the back of the article. It simply read...*
*"I am so proud to have a daughter who takes her dreams out of the box.*
*Love,*
*Mom"*

*The lesson was invaluable. It didn't matter if I failed, it only mattered that I tried.*

*Life energy is about being able to pick ourselves up, dust ourselves and our dreams off and keep on going.*

*Life energy is a two-way street. Have you given anyone an "energy transfusion" lately? That note from my mother was an "energy transfusion" for me.*

That pumped you up. But what happens when there isn't an "energy transfusion" and we "freeze?"

*What is it about the human being that our delivery of communication can be so situational? When we're presenting to a certain group we feel very comfortable. And yet with a different audience, we're not as confident. One of the things I've found with people in* *the corporate world is fear of "presenting up" — presenting to Senior Leaders. Examples might be a strategy presentation or annual operating plan presentation. In this case, we can become our own worst enemy. We <u>block</u> our own energy.*

That happens to me.

If John Madden is in the room, I become totally frozen. I guess it's like "presenting up" because he's at the top of my profession. I feel like there's a wall there. I know it's in my own head.

*Why do you think it's in your own head?*

Because I would love to get his approval without seeking it. I just feel like it's painful to speak when he's present. The microphone comes to me and it's almost difficult for me to speak. That's hard to realize for anybody who knows me.

*What about Terry Bradshaw? Do you feel that way about him?*

No. I can talk about anything with Terry Bradshaw.

*Why is there a difference with John Madden?*

I guess because in my mind, John is the elite. He's like the godfather of all broadcasters. His opinion is the only one that really matters.

It's hard to explain, but it's there, and it's paralyzing.

*Isn't it interesting that you and I have used the words "candid" and "blunt" to describe you Brian, and yet in this situation, you're not at all. You're completely at the other end of the scale.*

I'm comfortable talking to just about anyone. I could talk to a dead man and still make it interesting! So why does it feel so paralyzing? There are actually a couple of other people at Fox that have that same effect on me. When I do start to talk, I feel so stupid. I say the dumbest things. I never feel dumb talking to anybody else.

*What if you think of just enjoying the conversation instead of thinking you have to have their approval? Your perception is what I'm talking about. Not thinking at all about whether or not they approve of you. Take it out of the expressive circuit and put it into the receptive circuit. You just want to enjoy listening and learning from them.*

When I've taken that approach, I've found there were times when I really wanted to jump into the conversation, but I was hesitant. I didn't feel like I could speak with conviction so I didn't speak. I was able to sit back and enjoy listening, but I was still frustrated that I wasn't able to participate.

*That's a very interesting dynamic. What you're talking about is an energy-stopper. Something that just sucks the energy out of us.*

In my situation, what blocks me is always a person I put on some sort of pedestal. It's an intimidation. The result is that there is a complete energy loss.

*Anyone seeing you from the outside would say, "Nothing could take your energy away. You've got it all."*

I had an experience last week that made me understand more about my energy-stoppers. Another person I just couldn't talk to was

Randy White, Hall of Fame defensive tackle. I played with him for six years in Dallas and played against him every single day in practice. And yet at the end of the day I could never just sit down and talk to the guy.

I had this perception that I wasn't as good as he was. It was just fear, one big clump of fear.

But last week I was able to get through that fear. I was in New Orleans at the Saints' practice getting ready to do a game, and out of nowhere, Randy White walked into the building. I hadn't seen Randy in over a year, maybe two years. I found out that he was there to help the Saints with martial arts. He's a martial arts expert.

He came right up to me and said, "What's goin' on Baldinger? You down here doin' a game?"

He knows what I do! I said, "Big Guy," (I used to call him Big Guy). "Big Guy, what's happenin'?"

Then there was just a second, a moment, when I was thinking, "Am I going to fear this guy any more or am I going to walk right through it and eliminate the fear?"

I faced the fear and went right up to him and started talking to him. At the end, he said to me, "What are you doing for lunch?"

We went to a place in the French Quarter, and four hours went by before we finished lunch! Not only did we have an easy time talking with each other, Randy even gave me his mother's phone number. He told me to call her some time when I'm in the area. "Call Laverne. Go stop and see her."

Never again will I fear Randy White!

*So the fear you had created in your mind completely dissipated.*

Completely gone.

I talked with him one on one with no fear at all. He even complimented me on my broad-casting skills.

All the fear got sucked out of me.

And I'm going to go see his mom, too.

*What's going to happen the next time you're in a room with John Madden?*

That's the next domino that has to fall. John and I don't work on the same schedule, but at some point, we're going to cross paths, and I will just face the fear.

*This is behavior. It's walking through the fear. It's not letting fear be an energy-stopper.*

*Energy-stoppers can literally interfere with our lives. It's as though our feet are in cement, and we can't move forward.*

We can face the energy-stoppers and recognize what they are. Next time I experience that blockage, I'm going to say, "That's one of those energy-stoppers."

*Any time that you feel that force field, and you really want to say something, break the circuit. Ask yourself, "What do I really want to say or do right now?" Then, just do it.*

*Facing energy-stoppers is a major way we can get ourselves going. We can choose to fill our lives with energy.*

*It's taking a firm hold on the steering wheel, mapping out the journey and stepping on the gas pedal.*

*So ladies and gentlemen:*
- *J'arm (see bibliography)*
- *Laugh*
- *Believe*
- *Defeat energy-stoppers*
- *Edit out the toxic people, places, and things that deplete your energy*
- *And be congruent in your communication*

# Congruent Communication

There are three areas of Expressive Communication (the way we send messages):
1. the sounds and tones of our voice
2. the words we choose to use, and
3. our facial expressions and body language.

These are otherwise known as:
1. SPEECH
2. VERBAL LANGUAGE and
3. VISUAL LANGUAGE

All three must send the same message at the same time in order to effectively deliver the intended message. *That* is CONGRUENCY.

What happens when we're incongruent? If you start a meeting by saying, "I'm happy you're all here. We have some very important information to cover today." But you make no eye contact, are slouching, and have no **energy** or inflection in your voice, what message do you think people will "get"? The message they'll receive is that you're not happy at all and that this information can't possibly be that important. Studies show that the receiver's perception of the message is influenced most by our actions, secondly by our sounds and tones, and lastly by our words. (Mehrabian studies)

If you want your message to be clearly understood and not misinterpreted, make sure you use congruent communication. Send the same message with your voice and your body language that you are sending with your words! People will then feel your life energy.

**Post-Note**

A new book from Gallup confirms that energy and passion do pay off. In *"Follow This Path,"* Gallup argues that boosting morale can raise profits — by 40%.

Gallup's newest research found that most companies operate as if employees and customers were completely rational. "Not so" says Gonzalez-Molina. "We are first and foremost emotional beings. Our highest-level goals are set by emotion, not reason." By those lights, if you want charged-up employees and customers who love you, you have to grab 'em by the heart strings.

# Confident, Caring Coaching

I learned a long time ago that people don't care how much you know, until they know how much you care. This, in my opinion, is true in regard to coaching on any level. To efficiently and sincerely transmit a feeling that you do care about them as people as well as players, can only be communicated by direct contact. As long as you, as a coach, are controlling the topics, there is no way you can invest too much time talking with your players.

Now, you must realize, there is a big difference between talking and communicating. True communication takes place only after you have established credibility, and credibility isn't established until you are evaluated as being honest and sincere. These attributes are developed through direct communication with your team, and/or through your former players passing on positive feedback to those with whom they come in contact on your team.

Credibility travels fast if you have earned it, and if you haven't earned it, you can't utilize it as the foundation for your communicating game plan. It is not complicated. People complicate it.

> Dick Vermeil
> Winning Super Bowl Coach

*The coach has a responsibility to the individual and the organization or business. Coaches help people move to "next." Both personal best and personal next.*

*Great coaches also understand the organization/business and the alignment between what the individual needs to develop to achieve the desired outcomes of the organization/business.*

*Coaching is a piece of the bigger picture.*

*Nadine Udall Fischer*

## Confident, Caring Coaching

You know, Nadine, later in this book in the Wizard & Warrior chapter, we talk about how I came to you for coaching, and what I actually experienced. So, I think in this chapter, it's best if you just talk to us about some of your experiences. I've seen you be consistent in the way you approach coaching and the changes you've helped people make, including me.

*First, Brian, let me be specific about some of the leaders I've worked with. My experiences aren't only about coaching them, it's about some of the lessons I've learned from working with them.*

*Last week, when I met with Fred Poses, CEO of American Standard, we focused on two areas that I think are extremely important. First, Fred talked about how much we focus on our expressive language, and we need to be equally, if not more, focused on receptive communication. Great leaders are also great listeners. In coaching there are skill sets that we all can use to enhance people's ability to clearly receive messages. And then Fred and I talked about what's come to be known as the*

*"burning platform theory." That is, establishing a sense of urgency as to something that needs to be done immediately. In the coaching process, often there is an immediate need, an analyst meeting, an external presentation to a large group of people. But looking beyond that immediate sense of urgency, to being a great communicator, on an on-going basis, is the ultimate desired outcome for coaching. So the coach needs to have a balance between just-in-time coaching and coaching that has long-term lasting results.*

*Recently, I worked with Dave Weidman, the CEO of Celanese Chemicals, and the COO of Celanese A.G. We were preparing for a global leadership conference. Dave immediately saw the importance of an aligned message delivered by every single one of the leaders presenting at this conference. It wasn't about coaching one individual; it was about coaching an entire team around their performance at that conference. We worked together to ensure that the environment was right, the messages were clear, the energy sustained and created a defining moment for the company.*

*Ram Charan, co-author of the book* "Execution, the Discipline of Getting Things

Done", *was also a speaker at this conference. It was also important to spend time with Ram, prior to the conference, so that he understood the company, the issues and to ensure that his presentation fit into the larger picture.*

*The up-front process, the time invested in analyzing the situation, developing a plan of approach and then following through in terms of rehearsals, outstanding delivery and continuous follow-up after the leadership conference, was what made it a success. Coaching was a piece of the bigger picture.*

*People sometimes ask what I mean by emotional coaching. It's something that's hard to put your finger on. I once worked with a great leader, well respected by his team, but he had a lot of trepidation about "presenting up." As we were preparing for his strategy presentation to that group, he shared with me some of those concerns. I asked him a few questions. One of the things I knew about him, because of researching history, was that he was a respected and well-decorated pilot. And so I asked him, "Can anyone else fly a plane like you can? Has anyone else that will be in that room experienced being in control under the most difficult combat situations?"*

*His answer simply was "No."*

*And so I said to him, "When you get in that cockpit, you go through a checklist, and you have absolute confidence that you'll perform at the highest capability. When you walk into that room next week, you're the pilot and you have a checklist. You're going to feel the same confidence you have when you're in the cockpit, and your strategic mission is clear."*

*We mapped the message, rehearsed the presentation, and visualized this pilot's performance during the next week. The feedback he received was outstanding. It was interesting to see the change in his own physiology when he visually put himself in the cockpit.*

*Dr. Warren Wilhelm, President of Global Consulting Alliance, and I have worked on a number of leadership projects over the years. One of the most challenging missions we were ever given was to create understanding about the concept of cash flow within an entire company. The desired outcome was that every individual within the company understand how important cash flow is to the health of an organization and its long-term future. Making this complex communication simple, and coaching individuals to deliver the message, was our mission.*

*We chose the avenue of breaking the commu-nication into three distinct pieces. First, there would be a coached introduction by the indi-viduals who had been selected to be part of this program. The second piece was an ani-mated video presentation which simplified the concept of cash flow, looking at cash flow in terms of how it related to individuals, then a small business and finally within a very large corporation. The message was simple, easy to understand, and fun to receive.*

*The third piece was a recap of the concepts introduced in the video, time for questions and answers with great involvement by the audience in terms of how they could person-alize this, how it applies to their own life or their own business unit, where they were op-erating and living each day. The follow-up was a brief and concise survey asking partici-pants to recall the most important messages they received, and how they could personally contribute to improving cash flow at the company. Sometimes coaching becomes a piece of the overall strategic plan for effec-tive communication and the ability to create*

*understanding, even within what might ap-*
*pear to be a very complex communication.*

*And then there are times that we don't see*
*people as coaches because that's not what*
*they do for a living; but in reality, it's what*
*they do for a life.*

*I can think of one person, who at the ripe*
*young age of 18, went into the navy, served in*
*Europe and Asia, flew off of cruisers and air*
*craft carriers. He was shot down, but never*
*disheartened. I remember hearing about how*
*he catapulted off the ship, but also what it*
*took for the crew to land on the ship. After all,*
*this was over 50 years ago. His stories mes-*
*merized me, but it took him until he was in his*
*70s to be able to talk in detail about some of*
*those experiences. It was one of the most de-*
*fining moments in his life, yet one of the hard-*
*est to talk about.*

*A person of courage and of honor is so*
*needed in this day and age. This man of*
*honor carried that intuitive coaching with*
*him whether he was teaching Sunday School,*
*leading a youth group at church or raising*
*kids. Although this man never went to col-*
*lege, he had wisdom that was infinite, and,*

*with any person he touched, he wanted that person to be the best he or she could be.*

*Close to a decade ago, that man celebrated his 50th wedding anniversary, an accomplishment in and of itself.*

*Young people whose lives he had influenced (although they hadn't seen him in over 25 years) came to honor him and the love of his life.*

*He may not be the CEO of a Fortune company, he may not ever have coached a Super Bowl football team, but my father coached me, and for that I will be forever grateful.*

## Confident, Caring Coaching Tips

1. Trust. Develop a level of trust. The person you're working with needs to know you want the best for them. As a coach, you also need to be able to trust that they *want* to be coached and are engaged in the process.
2. Use E.Q. Coaching is as much emotional as it is affecting behavioral changes. The emotional quotient, using our intuitive relationship radar is critical.
3. History. It's important to inquire about, and understand the person's history. These are some questions to ask:

- How long have you been in your present position?
- What have your past responsibilities included?
- What are your current responsibilities?
- What are the types of presentations you've given in the past, and what do you anticipate for the future?
- What is your end goal? How do you see yourself as a communicator in the future? It is important to set clear expectations that both of you agree upon.

4. Environment and context. A coach needs to understand the climate of the business in which the person works. General overviews of the organization help a coach not only understand the business aspect, but also how the person fits into the organization.

5. Care. People need to know that you care and want them to achieve their coaching goals.

6. Listen. Communication is a two-way street. Not only do we need to use Expressive Language in our coaching, we also need to use Receptive Language skills. By truly listening for the obvious, as well as the hidden messages, we can develop solid coaching relationships.

7. Next. Always coach to "next." Don't focus on where someone isn't, or on the negative behaviors. Move their focus, through a modeling process, to a level of behavioral enhancement of the skills they are focusing on improving.

8. Don't over-coach. A coach focuses on the 3 or 4 behavioral changes that can give the most immediate return on the coaching investment. Focus on these until the person has internalized them, plateaus, and then moves onto the next level.
9. Every human being is unique; don't try to change that. Work within their individual style to make them the very best individual they can be. Trying to change style can make someone robotic and unauthentic. Respect individual differences. The objective is for them to be their personal best.
10. As a coach, you need to love what you do! People see that come through in your coaching. Have fun!

*Coaching is a two-way street, so here are some tips for the "coachee."*

## Coachee Tips

1. Make sure you feel comfortable with your coach. That relationship is vital. You may need to interview two or three coaches before you find the right one
2. Think about something you do really well. A moment when you had great success. Focus in on that experience.
3. Think about your history and how it affects the way you communicate.
4. If your company has a management review process, make sure the coaching aligns with your personal development plan.

5. Coaching is a two-way street. If you truly don't want to engage in the process, it just will not work.
6. Coaching is a reciprocal process. Make sure your coach consistently receives your feedback.
7. Be willing to practice new behaviors. Just as a great musician practices for a performance, or an athlete practices for a sport, to become a great communicator we need to be willing to work at it. It may be uncomfortable, but the more we practice, the more we internalize new behaviors.
8. Focus in on those behaviors you think will make the most difference in your performance. Then practice, practice, practice.
9. Be true to yourself. Remain your own, authentic, honest human being.
10. Enjoy the process. We recently worked with a chief legal counsel who broke into singing "Moon River" whenever he had the microphone in his hand. We loved it! Another leader was open to changing the contours of his voice, and so he practiced reading children's books out loud. These individuals "delighted" in the learning process.

**CARE** – A formula to keep in mind when coaching.

**C** Make a positive first contact and create a trustful, respectful coaching relationship.

**A** Ask, analyze, and aud. Auding is the most intense level of listening. It's when we are using <u>all</u> of our modalities. What does the individual need and expect? How does that align with the desired business outcomes?

**R** Remodel, rehearse, restate. Remodeling a communication behavior and then practicing that new behavior (rehearsal) is invaluable to coaching. Restate, consistently, the enhanced behavior pattern.

**E** Encourage, energize, execute. Great coaches motivate, and they also make certain that the new behaviors are executed.

*NOTE:*
Verbally demeaning or abusive language in any coaching situation is unacceptable.

# The Wizard and the Warrior

Nadine can take a very complex message or project, simplify it, then align, motivate and inspire the leaders of a company to communicate that message relentlessly.

Her skill is not just simplifying a message. She leaves such an imprint on the hearts and souls of leaders that every one of them wants to make a difference in the organization.

Warren Wilhelm
President
Global Consulting Alliance

*To be successful communicators, human beings need both an internal Wizard and Warrior. The Wizard has vision, insight, and intuition. The Gentle Warrior has courage, conviction, and strength.*

*Nadine Udall Fischer*

## The Wizard and the Warrior

*Brian, you've called me a Wizard and I've called you a Warrior, but why did we give each other those nicknames?*

When you and I met, we were such obvious opposites. You were warm and delightful. I was intense, passionate, and loud. The sound of our voices, our appearance and everything — it was just such a contrast. I was bullish, aggressive, and forceful — about everything.

*When you first came to the office and I was going to coach you, you had an attitude that came across as intimidating. I actually thought twice about working with you. But I knew you had to be really motivated or you never would have been seeking my advice.*

Remember, Nadine, that intimidation is a very important part of football. Football players take that exterior everywhere they go. Usually it's manufactured. Most football players aren't really like that. It's a quality that's necessary to have longevity in football. Somebody is always coming after your job, and your position is very tenuous from year to year. Health is always an issue, and you've got to present yourself as the "baddest" and strongest and toughest

individual on earth to ensure that you maintain that position from year to year. It's very difficult to just leave it on the field and not take it with you wherever you go.

*The offensive lineman mentality can really wear you out — always being ready to fight. You and I have talked about a different mentality, that of a Gentle Warrior who takes energy and makes it work positively. That's powerful.*

Somehow, without taking the Warrior qualities away from me, because those are good qualities in certain situations, you were able to soften up the interior and polish the exterior. People don't really want to see a sports broadcaster on television yelling at somebody. That's basically what I was doing. I was too forceful.

I had to learn how to change the tone of my voice. I was the Warrior, all right. I needed to learn what qualities would make me more effective on television.

*Was your Warrior a defense?*

I suppose it was, but it was a necessary one. When you and I met, I was still trying to play football. I hadn't, for a moment, thought my career was over. Even though I had played 13 *years, I was trying to play a 14th. That's just the mentality. I was dead set on doing it.*

*Did my advice help you make sense of your career path?*

At first, I wasn't really convinced of anything you were telling me. I was learning, and I thought maybe it would be good stuff down the road, but I wasn't actually buying it. I needed help on writing a speech and you were there to do that. But then I became amazed at the process, how you were able to just pull it all together from talking with me. That was interesting. But my mind was still on the field, all the way. It wasn't until later that year, when I officially announced my retirement, that I began to turn things around, and then what you were saying began to make sense.

*You and I had some pretty animated discussions about you retiring from football.*

I had this master plan that I wanted to play one more year. I thought I could develop strong relationships with the media while I was still playing and afterward move right into broadcasting. That was my plan. In the long run, I learned it doesn't make any difference. You were trying to tell me about life after football,

but I didn't start listening until the NFL wasn't listening to me. The NFL wasn't interested in a guy who had played 13 years and who had accumulated some major injuries.

*I recall there was a time you didn't feel your broadcasting career was moving along the way you wanted it to.*

I was getting frustrated. I was doing everything I thought was the right thing to do. I was volunteering, taking any job possible to get air time. I was looking for suggestions any place I could find them. Finally, I made some penetration into the local Philadelphia market, and I began sending tapes out to national affiliates, both radio and television. But I wasn't getting any response. None whatsoever. Not even a call back.

Then, I was trying to cultivate various agents, thinking they might be interested in helping me. But those people weren't calling me back either. Almost two years into this effort, I was ready to just hang it up. Ready to stop altogether. I was earning very little money even though I was working a great deal.

Really, it was just ego. I simply needed more

coaching and I had to be patient. That's what you kept trying to stress — how important patience was. If you believe in what you're doing, enjoy what you're doing, and work at what you're doing, it will eventually happen.

*When did things start to change for you?*

I went through a down period, for maybe a month or more, and then finally the phone started ringing with some opportunities. Pretty soon I just decided to stay on it, to give it another year, see what happens.

That next year, things really began to happen. I had expected immediate success, immediate responses from people. When people didn't return my phone calls, I thought it was rude, but that's just part of the behavior in business. They call you when they're ready. It was a great learning experience.

*What about the vision we talked about?*

At one point, you had a very clear vision of what you thought I could do. You saw more for me than I did, and you saw it happening more quickly than I thought it could happen. You were very convincing.

*You didn't seem convinced at the time. I can even remember where I was sitting when you were screaming at me that this wasn't ever going to happen.*

That was definitely a day my Warrior appeared.

*That was a day when I learned from you. I realized that I had always been understanding and empathetic with you when I was trying to guide you through things. But that's when you taught me about my Gentle Warrior. We had never talked about my personal life up to that point, had we?*

No, you were pretty quiet about that.

*I remember firmly saying to you, "You don't even have a clue what patience is. You played in sports and everybody fell all over you! Now, welcome to the real world! You are not the only person who has problems. Other people have difficulties, too. And sometimes it takes not days, not months — but decades for everything to come together."*

*There was something happening inside me when I stood up to you that day. My Gentle Warrior came out. When I shared my insights, my own personal experiences, and what I thought patience really meant, it was a defining moment for both of us. You sat back and thought, "Maybe there is something to this patience thing." And I discovered that there was a Gentle Warrior that lived inside of me, too.*

*That's what you taught me, that there's a time to stand up and draw the line. There are boundaries, and you have to just say, "Okay, stop now."*

I think you saw that everything could be balanced, that there is a place for being firm about what you're trying to get across. I possessed those qualities. I personified the Warrior.

*Having worked with you at that point for more than two years, I was learning that it is possible to stand firm and strong. Now, I can reach inside and be a Gentle Warrior when I need to be.*

Didn't you have this Gentle Warrior before then, even with all your corporate work?

*I know I had strength of character. Yes, I drew boundaries, but I certainly draw them a lot more clearly and quickly today.*

It's been a full circle for both of us.

*We have brought out the professional best in each other.*

For me, this whole process has been enlightening. I was successful as a football player, but I didn't know why I was successful. I just had this mindset that it was only hard work that got me there.

Now, I believe that there's a lot more than hard work. There's got to be an underlying belief in what you're doing and why you do it. You do it because you really like doing it, and that's why it works for you.

*A lot of people feel that the only way they can become successful is to be completely obsessed and driven. Brian, that's how you approached football and how you were beginning to approach your new career.*

I'm learning not to do that anymore. I believe I can be the best in this business of broadcasting, because it's something I enjoy doing.

*I remember telling you about a perspective I had for myself about "heart armor." I could put it on when I had to go into some tough corporate situations. I would put on my heart armor so I wouldn't lose my heart. It was a way to protect myself and be strong and focused in the corporate world, but I could quickly take the armor off for my children. I used that to help you understand yourself. I told you, "You've got your armor on all the time." You were holding back, and it came out like you were barking. My suggestion was to sometimes take that armor off and move from the grizzly bear to the teddy bear. That allowed you to bring great spirit to everything you do.*

You thought I should get a Labrador retriever and assume the personality of a Lab!

*I was trying to help you visualize.*

You even offered to go shopping for a puppy with me!

*I wanted to get you to soften up a little bit. That's how I help people visualize their behaviors and how to get there.*

It was a great analogy to get me to soften up. It wasn't necessary to be such a full time Warrior.

My journey to the top of the broadcasting

profession is very different from football. I don't have to put armor on all the time, if at all, as a matter of fact. People like to see others with all their warts, their frailties, and concerns. That just seems to make people a little more human, a little more whole, and everyone relates to that.

*And I don't put my "heart armor" on as often any more.*

As an analyst for professional football, I think people watching the game always want to hear more about the people who are playing. They're always looked at as being Warriors, and they're never really looked at as being warm or human. If you get to know these guys, there are some great stories to be told, and I think people in the audience would like to hear some of those.

*One of the greatest skills of leadership is the ability to storytell. It fascinates people. That's one of the strengths you bring to what you do. You're a wonderful storyteller. You get to know the players and coaches inside and out.*

The research behind the scenes is very important. I put a lot of time and effort into preparing by getting all the information I can. That's a crucial factor in the success of any presentation or broadcast. Don't you think?

*No question about it. Not only do I coach my executive clients to do that, I do it myself.*

I'll never forget your experience with the president of the World Boxing Union. When you called me up and told me he was a new client, I was excited because I've got a real love for the sweet science; that's what boxing is called, the sweet science. They had a big conference he was getting ready for, and he wasn't a confident public speaker. The World Boxing Union had had a successful year, and he wanted to kick off the conference in a way to celebrate that.

When you said you were working with him, I thought, "This is the craziest association I've heard of. Nadine knows nothing about boxing!"

I remember watching actual boxing matches on tapes with you even as we were getting ready for an entirely different corporate conference. You said, "I really want to understand boxing." You sat there and learned enough about the subject to be able to figure out what they

needed to do and the strategy they needed to employ to open their conference, all without getting caught up in too many details.

It seems like that's what happens in business. People get caught up in too many details, and they are never able to see the bigger picture about what they're *really* trying to accomplish. You have that ability. That's Nadine the Wizard!

You know, I can remember exactly when I decided you were a Wizard. It was an icy, snowy, winter day when you and I were meeting with a group in Atlantic City. You were involved in a car accident, and you probably should have been hospitalized, but you went to great lengths to get to the meeting, no matter what.

You battled through bad weather, and trying to find a replacement car, and flying into Atlantic City airport, and all kinds of other nonsense to get to this speech you had to make. I was amazed that somebody would not only be that dependable, but risk that kind of safety and then also deliver a great speech like nothing happened. You really had it all together.

*So a Wizard goes on no matter what obstacles appear?*

There must be some inner fortitude that keeps a Wizard going despite obstacles.

*What I've learned working with leaders is that leaders need to be both Wizards and Gentle Warriors. They have an inner sense of vision for the company and can draw the line clearly and quickly when the situation calls for it.*

*There's also a place for both of these roles in everyday life. Human beings have to be a balance of a Wizard and a Gentle Warrior. You can't be as successful without balancing the two of them.*

Is the Wizard inside all of us more than a little voice that tells us what to do?

*It's a solid feeling of knowing this is the right thing to do. The Wizard sees the big picture and has the ability to stay focused on it.*

You're a Wizard every time I watch you go into a corporate environment where it's a really difficult situation. When you work with a leadership team to simplify their business strategy so they can clearly communicate it to everyone, you're right there in the middle of it all. As you try to get people aligned and focused on what

needs to be done, somehow you're able to avoid all the arrows and all the egos. Somehow you see through it all. You always look at the bigger picture.

You're absolutely bullet proof. You're like smoke through a keyhole. You get into the tightest places and get the work done.

*As a Wizard and a Warrior, you and I make a good team. We complement each other and keep each other on track.*

If everyone could zero in on their own personal Wizard and Warrior, they would project an inner confidence that's a powerful tool in communicating.

*The Gentle Warrior has courage, conviction, and strength. The Wizard has vision, insight, and intuition.*

## Book Close

*So there it is...The Map.*

*First, check the language you think in.*

*Second, make sure the intent is pure.*

*Third, analyze the Four Factors.*

*Fourth, create a Message Map.*

*Fifth, Start Your Life Energy!*

*Sixth, know that you too, can be a confident, caring coach, and,*

*Seventh, discover that wonderful Wizard and Gentle Warrior that lives inside of you.*

*Good luck on your journey.*

# Note From the Authors

If there's anything both of us learned from creating this book, it's that nothing can replace face-to-face communication. In a high tech world, there is still plenty of room for the best way to communicate.

To be continued –

In our next conversation.

And we can't wait!

# Bibliography

Dr. Dale Anderson, *The Orchestra Conductor's Secret to Health and Long Life*, Chronimed Publishing, 1997.

Brian Billick, *Competitive Leadership: Twelve Principles for Success*, Triumph Books, 2001.

Larry Bossidy & Ram Charan, *Execution: The Discipline of Getting Things Done*, Crown Business, 2002.

Curt Coffman & Gabriel Gonzalez-Molina, Ph.D., *Follow This Path: How the World's Greatest Organizations Drive Growth by Unleashing Human Potential*, Warner Books, 2002.

Loy McGinnis, *Bringing Out the Best In People*, Augsburg Publishing House, 1985.

Robert McKee and Bronwyn Fryer, *Storytelling That Moves People*, Harvard Business Review, June 2003, Product # R0306B.

David Shenk, *Data Smog: Surviving the Information Glut*, Harper Edge, 1997.

129

# Bibliography

*Steve Wall & Harvey Arden, Wisdom KeepersBe-yond Words Publishing Inc., 1990.*

# To Contact

## Communications, LLC

*For Keynote/Capnote Presentations or*

*Executive Communication Coaching*

## Our Workshops:

*The Map to Clear Messages*

*Powerful Presentation Skills*

*Communicating on Camera*
*(The Camera Loves Ya Babe!)*

*Please call: 1-609-844-7541*


## Visit our websites:
## www.themaptoclearmessages.com
## www.nadiacommunications.com